VAN GOGH UNVEILED

From Starry Nights to Sunflowers

Exploring the Masterpieces of a Tortured Genius

Within the pages of this book, you will discover:

• A curated collection of 70 paintings by the masterful Vincent van Gogh, each selected for their artistic and historical significance.

• Brief commentary accompanying each piece, encompassing:

- Artwork Description - unveiling the visual splendor and technical aspects of each painting.
- Historical Context - providing insight into the circumstances of each work's creation.
- Symbolism and Interpretation - delving into the deeper meanings and artistic expressions.
- Critical Reception and Legacy - examining the impact and lasting influence of van Gogh's work on art and culture.
- Unique or Interesting Facts - revealing lesser-known details that enrich the understanding of van Gogh's artistic journey.

Exploring the Vibrant World of Vincent van Gogh

Welcome to "Beyond The Starry Night: The World of Vincent van Gogh," a vivid exploration into the life and legacy of one of the most influential artists in history. Vincent van Gogh, a name synonymous with artistic genius and emotional profundity, painted not just canvases, but stories – stories of struggle, passion, and an undying love for the act of creation. In this collection, we delve into the essence of Van Gogh's art, bringing to light the vibrant colors, bold textures, and profound emotions that define his work.

Born into a world that was not yet ready to embrace his unique vision, Van Gogh's life was a mosaic of intense highs and profound lows. His journey was one of a restless spirit searching for meaning through his art. In these pages, we trace his footsteps – from the wheat fields of Arles to the asylum of Saint-Rémy, each painting a chapter of his tumultuous life story. Van Gogh's art was more than just a visual experience; it was an emotional odyssey, and through this book, we invite you to journey through his most intimate moments.

This book aims to bridge the gap between Van Gogh the legend and Van Gogh the man. It is an invitation to understand his world, to see what he saw, feel what he felt. His works, celebrated for their raw, emotional power and revolutionary use of color, broke new ground in the world of art. Here, we present them not just as paintings, but as windows into the soul of a man who transformed personal turmoil into eternal beauty.

As you immerse yourself in these pages, we encourage you to look beyond the brushstrokes. Discover the stories behind each masterpiece, the symbolism rooted in every hue, and the legacy that Van Gogh left behind. This book is not just a collection of images; it is a narrative of an artist who poured his heart into every stroke, an artist who continues to inspire and captivate generations.

Finally, as you embark on this journey through Van Gogh's world, let his life be a testament to the enduring power of art. Despite facing numerous challenges, including mental illness and poverty, Van Gogh's work continues to resonate with millions around the globe. His legacy is a reminder that art is not just about creating beauty but about conveying the deepest human emotions and experiences. Welcome to a journey of discovery, emotion, and unparalleled artistry – the world of Vincent van Gogh.

At Eternity's Gate (1890)

Artwork Description:
"At Eternity's Gate" is a powerful portrayal of an elderly man, who is captured in a moment of despair as he sits with his head in his hands. The figure is enveloped in a blue smock, which contrasts with the warm tones of the wooden chair and floor. Van Gogh's use of thick, emotive brushstrokes intensifies the subject's emotional state, inviting viewers to a profound empathy.

Historical Context:
This work was created during the final months of Van Gogh's life, a period when he was grappling with severe depression. The piece reflects Van Gogh's own psychological turmoil and his empathy for the human condition. The subject is thought to be an inhabitant of the asylum in Saint-Rémy where Van Gogh was staying.

Symbolism and Interpretation:
The title "At Eternity's Gate" suggests a contemplation of mortality and the spiritual journey. The pose of the man, with his face buried in his hands, is often interpreted as a universal symbol of sorrow. The painting can be seen as Van Gogh's meditation on human suffering and perseverance through life's trials.

Critical Reception and Legacy:
Van Gogh's work was not widely recognized during his lifetime, but posthumously, he became one of the most influential figures in Western art history. "At Eternity's Gate" is particularly notable for its raw emotional impact and is often seen as a precursor to expressionist art.

Unique or Interesting Facts:
Van Gogh created several drawings with similar themes before this painting, reflecting his long-standing interest in the subject of human endurance in the face of hardship. The painting is said to have been inspired by a lithograph that Van Gogh made in 1882 called "Worn Out," which depicts an old man, exhausted, with his head in his hands.

Almond Blossom (1890)

Artwork Description:
"Almond Blossoms" by Vincent van Gogh is a stunning depiction of the blooming almond trees against a clear blue sky. The branches are rendered with expressive, curving lines, while the blossoms are highlighted with impasto touches of white and pale pink. The contrast between the vitality of the flowering branches and the serene blue background creates a sense of renewal and life.

Historical Context:
Van Gogh painted "Almond Blossoms" in Saint-Rémy-de-Provence in 1890, shortly before his death. This period was marked by both intense creativity and debilitating mental health crises for the artist. The flowering almond tree, a sign of early spring and new life, was a subject that Van Gogh revisited multiple times, inspired by the Japanese prints he admired.

Symbolism and Interpretation:
Almond blossoms symbolize hope and awakening, which were likely appealing to Van Gogh during his stay at the asylum in Saint-Rémy. They were also emblematic of new life, corresponding to the birth of his nephew, named Vincent after him. The painting was a gift to his brother Theo and sister-in-law Jo, in celebration of the birth.

Critical Reception and Legacy:
While Van Gogh did not live to see the widespread acclaim his work would achieve, "Almond Blossoms" has become one of his most beloved pieces, appreciated for its beauty and vitality. It exemplifies Van Gogh's influence on the development of modern art, particularly with its bold colors and emotional resonance.

Unique or Interesting Facts:
A fact that adds a touching personal dimension to the painting is that Van Gogh created it for his newborn nephew, as a symbol of new beginnings. This personal connection may have imbued the work with an extra layer of care and meaning, as it was intended to hang above the child's crib, representing the new life of his namesake.

Avenue of the Plane Trees near Arles Station (1888)

Artwork Description:
"Avenue of the Plane Trees near Arles Station" depicts a row of robust plane trees casting vibrant shadows upon the ground, with the railway station of Arles in the background. The scene is painted with thick, vivid brushstrokes, typical of Van Gogh's style, and the palette is rich with yellows and blues, reflecting the southern light and the seasonal changes in the foliage.

Historical Context:
This painting was created in 1888 when Van Gogh lived in Arles, a period during which he produced some of his most famous works. The railway station was a modern symbol of progress and movement, and its inclusion in the painting reflects the changing landscape of the time.

Symbolism and Interpretation:
Plane trees are often symbols of longevity and resilience, and their presence here might reflect Van Gogh's search for stability and permanence amidst his own turbulent emotions. The avenue leading towards the station could also symbolize a journey, both literally and metaphorically, highlighting themes of transition and passage.

Critical Reception and Legacy:
While Van Gogh was not widely recognized during his lifetime, his works, including this painting, gained significant critical acclaim after his death. Today, Van Gogh is celebrated as a master of Post-Impressionism, and his paintings have inspired countless artists and art lovers.

Unique or Interesting Facts:
Van Gogh was fascinated by the changing light and seasons and often painted the same scenes at different times to capture these variations. "Avenue of the Plane Trees near Arles Station" is part of a series that explores this theme, showcasing his remarkable ability to depict light and shadow.

Bedroom in Arles (1888)

Artwork Description:
"Bedroom in Arles" is a vivid portrayal of Van Gogh's bedroom in the Yellow House in Arles, France. The painting is known for its bright colors and perspective that seems to flatten the room, providing a sense of tranquility and simplicity. The furniture and personal items in the room are rendered with care, offering a glimpse into the artist's living space.

Historical Context:
Van Gogh painted this work during a period of optimism before the arrival of Paul Gauguin, with whom he hoped to establish an artist's colony. The room represented a place of refuge and peace for Van Gogh, contrasting with his tumultuous emotional life.

Symbolism and Interpretation:
The simplified style and use of color in "Bedroom in Arles" reflect Van Gogh's desire for rest and order. The artwork has been interpreted as an embodiment of the artist's search for serenity amidst the chaos of his mind. The bright yellow of the bed and walls contrasts with the blue of the doors and windows, symbolizing warmth and comfort.

Critical Reception and Legacy:
While the painting was not widely known during Van Gogh's lifetime, it has since become one of his most beloved works, admired for its bold color scheme and intimate insight into his life. It is often seen as a precursor to modern interior paintings.

Unique or Interesting Facts:
Van Gogh created three versions of the "Bedroom in Arles," each with slight variations in color and detail. He considered the painting to have a special significance, as it conveyed his ideal of a simple life. The room itself, located in the Yellow House, became an iconic subject in art history, representing Van Gogh's artistic sanctuary.

Self-Portrait (1889)

Artwork Description:
In this self-portrait, Van Gogh depicts himself with an intense and penetrating gaze. The swirling patterns in the background are reminiscent of his iconic "Starry Night" and create a dynamic contrast with the more traditionally rendered figure. The green jacket and the reddish beard highlight Van Gogh's use of complementary colors.

Historical Context:
Van Gogh painted this self-portrait after his release from the hospital in Saint-Rémy-de-Provence, where he admitted himself after suffering from mental health issues. The painting reflects his psychological state and his mastery of Post-Impressionist techniques.

Symbolism and Interpretation:
The swirling background often is interpreted as a representation of the artist's inner turmoil or the chaos of the creative mind. Self-portraits were a way for Van Gogh to express and understand his condition and his identity.

Critical Reception and Legacy:
Today, Van Gogh's self-portraits are among his most famous works, celebrated for their emotional depth and striking color palettes. This particular piece is noted for its raw emotional expression and is often seen as an embodiment of the artist's troubled psyche.

Unique or Interesting Facts:
Van Gogh's use of a swirling background was unique to his self-portraits and is not found in those of his contemporaries. This distinctive style has contributed to the ongoing fascination with his work and his reputation as a pioneer of expressionism.

The Bridges at Asnières (1887)

Artwork Description:
"The Bridges at Asnières" by Vincent van Gogh depicts a scene along the Seine River, with the industrial bridges of Asnières in the background. Van Gogh's use of bright, contrasting colors and structured brushstrokes captures the reflection of the sunlight off the water and the vibrancy of the summer day. The figures in the painting add a human element to the industrial landscape, creating a contrast between nature, humanity, and the burgeoning industrial era.

Historical Context:
This painting was created during Van Gogh's time in Paris, a period when he was exposed to the works of the Impressionists and began incorporating their brighter palette and lighter brushwork into his art. The scene reflects the modernization of Paris and its outskirts during the late 19th century, a subject of fascination for many artists of the time.

Symbolism and Interpretation:
Bridges in Van Gogh's work can be seen as symbols of connection and transition. In this painting, the bridges may represent the link between the natural world and the industrial progress of the time. The inclusion of the lone figure with the red parasol could symbolize individuality amid the expanding urban environment.

Critical Reception and Legacy:
While Van Gogh's work received little attention during his lifetime, his posthumous recognition has been profound. "The Bridges at Asnières" is now celebrated for its innovative technique and its role in the evolution of Van Gogh's style. It contributes to our understanding of his development as an artist and his exploration of color and light.

Unique or Interesting Facts:
"The Bridges at Asnières" is part of a series of paintings that Van Gogh made while experimenting with the techniques of the Pointillists, whom he had met in Paris. However, instead of adopting their method completely, Van Gogh used it to develop his own unique style, characterized by dynamic and expressive brushstrokes. This painting is a key example of his transitional phase, merging new influences with his distinctive approach.

Blossoming Chestnut Branches (1890)

Artwork Description:
"Blossoming Chestnut Branches" is a vibrant depiction of a cluster of chestnut tree branches in bloom. Vincent van Gogh's dynamic brushwork enlivens the white blossoms and lush green leaves, while the intense blue background adds depth and contrast. The thick application of paint, characteristic of Van Gogh's style, gives the composition a palpable texture.

Historical Context:
Created in 1890, during the final year of Van Gogh's life, this painting belongs to a series of floral studies that he undertook while at the asylum in Saint-Rémy-de-Provence. The focus on nature and growth was typical of Van Gogh's work during this period, as he found solace and a sense of stability in the natural world.

Symbolism and Interpretation:
The blossoming chestnut branches may symbolize new life and hope, themes that were particularly meaningful to Van Gogh during his time of personal turmoil. The exuberant growth of the chestnut flowers could be read as an expression of resilience and the possibility of renewal.

Critical Reception and Legacy:
While Van Gogh was not widely recognized during his lifetime, his works have posthumously become some of the most celebrated in art history. "Blossoming Chestnut Branches" contributes to Van Gogh's legacy as an artist who profoundly impacted the course of modern art, particularly through his emotive use of color and innovative brushwork.

Unique or Interesting Facts:
Floral subjects like these offered Van Gogh an opportunity to experiment with color and technique without the pressure of creating a "serious" genre painting. This work, with its intense color contrasts and expressive handling of paint, reflects Van Gogh's evolving artistic style and his enduring influence on the art movements that followed.

Café Terrace at Night (1888)

Artwork Description:
"Café Terrace at Night" depicts a vibrant scene of a café in Arles, France. The painting is illuminated by the warm glow of the café's lighting against the deep blue of the starlit sky. Van Gogh's use of contrasting colors creates a lively atmosphere, while the strong verticals and horizontals lend structure to the composition. The cobblestone pavement is rendered with dashes of color that suggest the bustling energy of the location.

Historical Context:
Van Gogh painted "Café Terrace at Night" after moving to Arles in search of the bright colors and light of the south of France. This period was one of the most productive and innovative times in his career, as he began experimenting with the night effects and starry skies that would become a hallmark of his later work.

Symbolism and Interpretation:
Van Gogh often found meaning in the night sky, which he saw as a symbol of infinity and the divine. The café scene could be interpreted as a place of human connection and earthly comforts, juxtaposed with the vast and mysterious universe above.

Critical Reception and Legacy:
While Van Gogh's work was not widely recognized during his lifetime, "Café Terrace at Night" has become one of his most celebrated paintings. It is a testament to his revolutionary use of color and light, and it helped lay the groundwork for the development of Expressionism in the early 20th century.

Unique or Interesting Facts:
Van Gogh wrote to his sister that he was trying to express the idea that the café is a place where one can ruin oneself, go mad, or commit a crime. However, instead of depicting the café in a negative light, he paints it as a cozy, inviting space, filled with the warmth of human interaction. The café still exists and is a popular tourist destination, known as the Café Van Gogh.

Church of Auvers (1890)

Artwork Description:
"The Church at Auvers" is a vivid portrayal of the church in Auvers-sur-Oise, where Vincent van Gogh spent the last few months of his life. The painting is renowned for its swirling skies, the unconventional use of color, and its slightly askew perspective that distorts the church's actual architectural lines. The use of thick, expressive brushstrokes and vibrant colors are characteristic of Van Gogh's style during this period.

Historical Context:
Van Gogh painted "The Church at Auvers" in 1890 after committing himself to an asylum in Saint-Rémy-de-Provence. The church, part of the landscape that surrounded him in his final days, is a subject that reflects both his emotional turmoil and his artistic innovation during this period.

Symbolism and Interpretation:
The painting has been subject to various interpretations regarding its symbolism. Some suggest that the lack of a clear path leading to the church door signifies Van Gogh's troubled relationship with organized religion. The vivid colors and dramatic style have been interpreted as expressions of Van Gogh's personal feelings of isolation and despair.

Critical Reception and Legacy:
While Van Gogh was not commercially successful during his lifetime, his work received critical acclaim after his death. "The Church at Auvers" has been admired for its emotive strength and is considered one of his most evocative pieces. It exemplifies his contribution to the foundation of modern art.

Unique or Interesting Facts:
An interesting fact about this painting is that it does not depict the actual colors of the church; Van Gogh chose to use his palette to express his feelings rather than to render a realistic image. The painting is also often discussed in the context of Van Gogh's mental health, with some speculating that the swirling sky reflects his inner turmoil.

Portrait of Postman Joseph Roulin (1888)

Artwork Description:
This vibrant work features the postman Joseph Roulin, a close friend of Vincent van Gogh, seated and dressed in his blue postal uniform adorned with golden buttons and a matching cap with the word "POSTES." His striking beard and warm, direct gaze are characteristic features that Vincent captured with empathy and character.

Historical Context:
Joseph Roulin was one of Vincent's most frequent sitters during his time in Arles. The Roulin family became a subject of a series of portraits by Van Gogh, which illustrates the close relationship they shared.

Symbolism and Interpretation:
Van Gogh's portraits of Roulin are celebrated for their emotional depth. The postman's friendly and calm demeanor in the portrait symbolizes the comfort and stability he provided to Vincent during his turbulent life.

Critical Reception and Legacy:
The series of paintings featuring the Roulin family is considered some of Van Gogh's most important work. They exemplify his unique style and use of color during his Arles period.

Unique or Interesting Facts:
Van Gogh sought to capture the essence of his subjects by portraying them in their natural environments or in attire that reflected their daily lives. Joseph Roulin, the reliable postman, was a cherished friend, and this friendship is immortalized in these portraits.

Coal Brges (1888)

Artwork Description:
"Coal Barges" by Vincent van Gogh is a dynamic composition capturing the gritty reality of industrial life along the rivers of France. This painting is characterized by its bold use of color and vigorous brushwork, depicting the laborers at work with a backdrop of a vibrant, almost fiery sunset that reflects off the water's surface.

Historical Context:
Van Gogh painted "Coal Barges" during his time in Arles, in the south of France, a period when he was deeply influenced by the light and color of the region. This work is part of a series that reflects his interest in the lives of common people and the working class.

Symbolism and Interpretation:
The coal barges, as a subject, symbolize the industrialization of France during the late 19th century. Van Gogh's choice to depict this scene could be interpreted as an acknowledgment of the changing landscape and the hard labor that fueled the era's progress.

Critical Reception and Legacy:
While Van Gogh was not widely recognized during his lifetime, his posthumous recognition skyrocketed. "Coal Barges" contributes to the narrative of Van Gogh as an artist who was able to find beauty in everyday life and labor. His work has influenced countless artists and continues to be celebrated in modern times.

Unique or Interesting Facts:
A remarkable aspect of "Coal Barges" is Van Gogh's ability to convey motion through his brushstrokes, capturing the bustling activity of the workers. Additionally, this painting, like many of his works, did not achieve fame until after Van Gogh's death, at which point it helped to cement his legacy as a master of post-impressionism.

Congregation Leaving the Reformed Church in Nuenen (1884-85)

Artwork Description:
This work depicts parishioners departing from a church service in Nuenen, where Van Gogh's father was a minister. The church, a central structure in the composition, is somberly colored, and the figures are painted in a style that conveys the rustic character of the Dutch peasantry. The bare trees and overcast sky contribute to the painting's subdued atmosphere.

Historical Context:
Van Gogh painted "Congregation Leaving the Reformed Church in Nuenen" while living in Nuenen, where he focused on peasant life and landscapes. It reflects his Dutch artistic roots and his focus on the lives of common people.

Symbolism and Interpretation:
The church as the focal point symbolizes the central role of religion in rural life. The painting's muted colors and the solemn procession of figures may reflect Van Gogh's complex relationship with religion and his contemplation of mortality and the human condition.

Critical Reception and Legacy:
During Van Gogh's lifetime, his work was not widely recognized, and it was only after his death that his art gained significant critical attention. This painting, like many others, has contributed to the understanding of Van Gogh's early artistic development and his deep connection to the themes of rural life and religion.

Unique or Interesting Facts:
Van Gogh's choice to depict the church in Nuenen is personally significant, as his father was the pastor there. In 1885, Van Gogh added the group of churchgoers in the foreground, which may have included his father, to give the scene more life. The painting is also known for being stolen in a high-profile theft from the Van Gogh Museum in Amsterdam in 2002 and was recovered in Italy in 2016.

Cypresses (1889)

Artwork Description:
"Cypresses" by Vincent van Gogh is a striking depiction of the towering and robust cypress trees under a swirling Provençal sky. The painting is known for its intense hues and dramatic, energetic brushstrokes that convey the texture and movement of the foliage and the sky.

Historical Context:
Van Gogh created "Cypresses" during his stay at the Saint-Paul-de-Mausole asylum in Saint-Rémy-de-Provence. This period was one of great productivity for Van Gogh, despite the mental health challenges he faced. The cypress trees, common in the region, captured his interest, and he painted them several times.

Symbolism and Interpretation:
Cypress trees often symbolize death and the eternal, which may reflect Van Gogh's state of mind. The swirling sky and the lively, almost flame-like depiction of the trees have been interpreted as a reflection of Van Gogh's inner turmoil and his intense perception of the world around him.

Critical Reception and Legacy:
"Cypresses" was not widely known during Van Gogh's lifetime but has since become one of his most celebrated works, exemplifying his innovative style that has influenced the Expressionist movement. Today, the painting is considered a masterwork of Post-Impressionism.

Unique or Interesting Facts:
Van Gogh was fascinated by the cypress trees, which he said were "as beautiful of line and proportion as an Egyptian obelisk." He also mentioned that the cypresses were constantly in his thoughts, akin to the stars in his famous "Starry Night" painting. This obsession is reflected in the prominence and recurring theme of cypresses in his work from this period.

Edge of a Wheat Field with Poppies (1887)

Artwork Description:
This painting is a striking example of Van Gogh's fascination with nature and agricultural scenes. The foreground is dominated by golden wheat and red poppies, with trees and a blue sky filling the background. The brushwork is energetic and textured, with the poppies providing bursts of color against the wheat.

Historical Context:
Created during Van Gogh's time in Paris, this work reflects the influence of Impressionism on his style. During this period, he experimented with lighter colors and new brushstroke techniques, as seen in the depiction of the wheat field's movement and the vibrant poppies.

Symbolism and Interpretation:
Fields were a recurring theme in Van Gogh's work, symbolizing the cycles of life and nature's transient beauty. The contrast between the poppies and the wheat may represent the fleeting moments of life amidst the enduring rhythms of the natural world.

Critical Reception and Legacy:
Van Gogh's work received little recognition during his lifetime, but his approach to color and form had a profound impact on the development of modern art. His field paintings, including this one, are now celebrated for their innovative technique and emotional depth.

Unique or Interesting Facts:
Van Gogh often painted en plein air (outdoors), directly observing his subjects. This practice was integral to the Impressionists and Post-Impressionists. "Edge of a Wheat Field with Poppies" embodies his direct engagement with the landscape, capturing the scene's vitality and immediacy.

Fishing in Spring, the Pont de Clichy (Asnières) (1887)

Artwork Description:
"Fishing in Spring, the Pont de Clichy (Asnières)" is a painting by Vincent van Gogh that captures a serene moment of a man fishing by the banks of the Seine. The use of light and shadow, the reflection of the trees on the water, and the fresh greenery signify the renewal of spring. Van Gogh's brushwork is meticulous, with the dappled effects on the water and foliage adding a sense of vibrancy to the scene.

Historical Context:
Painted in 1887, this work was created during Van Gogh's time in Paris when he was heavily influenced by the Impressionists and Japanese prints. This period was significant for Van Gogh's artistic development, as he began experimenting with lighter colors, distinctive brushstrokes, and exploring the effects of light.

Symbolism and Interpretation:
The theme of a solitary figure in nature can be seen as a reflection of Van Gogh's own feelings of isolation. The act of fishing, often considered meditative, might symbolize a search for sustenance, peace, or meaning. The bridge, a common motif in art, could represent transition or connection between different states or places.

Critical Reception and Legacy:
Van Gogh's work was largely unappreciated during his lifetime, but his artistic genius was recognized posthumously. This painting is one of the many that show his transition from the darker Dutch palette to the brighter colors for which he is known. It's a testament to his evolving style and has helped solidify his status as a master painter.

Unique or Interesting Facts:
A notable aspect of this painting is Van Gogh's use of the Pointillist technique, which he adopted from artists like Seurat and Signac. Instead of fully embracing Pointillism, he used it to add texture and luminosity to his work, making it a bridge between traditional Impressionism and his unique style. This painting is also a reflection of Van Gogh's increasing interest in capturing the ephemeral effects of light and color, a focus that would come to define his later work.

Self-Portrait with Bandaged Ear and Pipe (1889)

Artwork Description:
In this self-portrait, Van Gogh depicts himself with his ear bandaged, after the infamous incident in which he mutilated his own ear. He is seen with a solemn expression, smoking a pipe. The red background contrasts sharply with the black coat and the fur-lined cap, emphasizing the artist's face.

Historical Context:
This self-portrait was painted shortly after Van Gogh's release from the hospital in Arles, where he was admitted after the ear-cutting episode. The event marked one of the most tumultuous periods in Van Gogh's life, deeply affected by psychological distress.

Symbolism and Interpretation:
Van Gogh's self-portraits are often seen as narrative windows into his state of mind. This work, with the inclusion of the pipe and the intense gaze, could be interpreted as a sign of the artist's attempt to return to normal life and work despite his ongoing struggles.

Critical Reception and Legacy:
Van Gogh's self-portraits are lauded for their emotional depth and raw honesty. This particular painting is often discussed for its stark portrayal of the artist's pain and isolation. It remains a powerful symbol of his battle with mental illness.

Unique or Interesting Facts:
Despite his condition, Van Gogh continued to produce a remarkable body of work during his recovery. His use of vibrant colors and the emotive force of his brushwork in this painting convey a complex inner world. The self-portrait is a testament to his resilience and dedication to art.

Bouquet of Flowers in a Vase (1890)

Artwork Description:
"Bouquet of Flowers in a Vase" by Vincent van Gogh features a lush array of flowers in an ornate vase. The painting bursts with a variety of colors and textures, showcasing Van Gogh's signature style of thick, expressive brushstrokes. The flowers are set against a dark background, which makes the vibrant colors of the petals stand out, creating a striking contrast.

Historical Context:
This painting was created in the last year of Van Gogh's life, a period when he was prolific in his work, despite battling severe bouts of mental illness. Van Gogh often painted flowers during his time in the asylum in Saint-Rémy-de-Provence, finding solace in the beauty and complexity of nature.

Symbolism and Interpretation:
Flowers were a common subject in Van Gogh's work, often representing growth, renewal, and the transient nature of life. In the context of Van Gogh's mental state at the time, the vibrant life in the flowers could symbolize moments of clarity and peace amid his personal turmoil.

Critical Reception and Legacy:
While Van Gogh sold only a few paintings in his lifetime and was not widely recognized, his work is now celebrated for its emotional depth and innovative technique. "Bouquet of Flowers in a Vase" contributes to his legacy, celebrated for its raw beauty and emotional resonance.

Unique or Interesting Facts:
Van Gogh's floral paintings have become some of his most famous works, appreciated for their vivid color and dynamic composition. Despite his troubled life, these works are a testament to his ability to capture the beauty of the world around him. "Bouquet of Flowers in a Vase" reflects his continuous experimentation with new styles and techniques, contributing to the evolution of his artistic legacy.

Flowering Garden (1888)

Artwork Description:
"Flowering Garden" by Vincent van Gogh is a vibrant canvas filled with rich textures and a multitude of colors that reflect a garden in full bloom. With a dynamic and almost tactile application of paint, Van Gogh conveys the wild and untamed beauty of the natural landscape.

Historical Context:
Created during his time in Arles in 1888, this painting is part of Van Gogh's exploration of the French countryside's light and color. His time in Arles was one of his most prolific periods, where he developed a brighter, more colorful palette influenced by the Provençal sun.

Symbolism and Interpretation:
Gardens often symbolize growth, rejuvenation, and nature's cycles, which may have resonated with Van Gogh during a period of recovery and artistic exploration. The garden's bursting life could be seen as a metaphor for creative potential and emotional expression.

Critical Reception and Legacy:
While Van Gogh was not commercially successful during his lifetime, "Flowering Garden" contributes to the body of work that would posthumously establish his reputation as a master of color and a forerunner of Expressionism. His garden paintings, in particular, are celebrated for their emotional depth and innovative technique.

Unique or Interesting Facts:
Van Gogh's garden paintings are noted for their absence of human figures, focusing instead on the landscape itself as the subject. This approach allows the viewer to engage directly with the natural environment, reflecting Van Gogh's desire to express the essence of his subjects through color and form. Additionally, his use of contrasting colors in this painting is a direct application of color theory, which he studied intensely, to enhance the vibrancy and emotional impact of the scene.

Path in the Woods (1887)

Artwork Description:
"Path in the Woods" showcases Vincent van Gogh's unique ability to capture the vibrancy of nature through his use of color and brushstroke. The painting is filled with a multitude of green hues, reflecting the varied textures and light within a forest setting. The path, which draws the viewer's eye into the scene, is rendered with a lighter touch, suggesting sunlight filtering through the canopy.

Historical Context:
Completed in 1887, this painting comes from Van Gogh's time in Paris when he was under the influence of the Impressionists and absorbing their interest in light and color. This period was crucial in his development as he began to break away from the darker palette of his early works.

Symbolism and Interpretation:
Paths through forests are often symbolic of journeys, both physical and metaphorical, and this could reflect Van Gogh's personal and artistic search for direction and meaning. The forest can also be seen as a place of introspection and solitude, themes that resonate with Van Gogh's own life.

Critical Reception and Legacy:
During his lifetime, Van Gogh struggled for recognition, but his work later garnered critical acclaim and has greatly influenced the art world. "Path in the Woods" contributes to his legacy as an artist who could convey intense emotion and movement through his depictions of the natural world.

Unique or Interesting Facts:
Van Gogh's forest scenes are less common than his famous fields and starry nights, making "Path in the Woods" a unique piece within his oeuvre. It also demonstrates his transition from the traditional Dutch artistic style to a brighter, more expressive palette influenced by his surroundings and the contemporary art movements of the time.

Sunflowers (1889)

Artwork Description:
"Sunflowers" is part of a famous series of paintings by Vincent van Gogh featuring robust, blooming sunflowers in a vase. The painting is notable for its vibrant yellow hues which dominate the composition, and its textured application of paint, which gives a lively, almost three-dimensional quality to the sunflowers.

Historical Context:
Van Gogh painted the "Sunflowers" series in Arles, France, in 1888 and 1889. These works were created during a period of heightened emotion and creativity for Van Gogh, which also coincided with the time he spent with Paul Gauguin. The sunflowers were intended, in part, to decorate Gauguin's room in the Yellow House they shared.

Symbolism and Interpretation:
Sunflowers were significant to Van Gogh; they symbolized gratitude and were meant to convey a message of welcome and friendship to Gauguin. They also represent the cycle of life and death, with some blooms standing tall and others wilting, which is often seen as a reflection of Van Gogh's preoccupation with mortality.

Critical Reception and Legacy:
While Van Gogh's "Sunflowers" received little attention during his lifetime, they are now among his most famous works, celebrated for their bold color and emotional depth. They are regarded as some of the most iconic images in Western art, symbolizing the movement toward modernism.

Unique or Interesting Facts:
Van Gogh created multiple versions of the "Sunflowers" with varying backgrounds and numbers of flowers, each one unique in its composition and expression. These paintings were among the first in Western art to use color for its symbolic and emotional value, rather than for realism. Additionally, "Sunflowers" are unique for their absence of human subjects, focusing solely on the beauty and complexity of nature.

Garden of the Hospital in Arles (1889)

Artwork Description:
"Garden of the Hospital in Arles" is a depiction of tranquility and peace found within the confines of a hospital garden. Van Gogh's use of vivid colors and bold strokes brings the garden to life, with the architectural elements of the hospital providing a structured backdrop to the natural forms.

Historical Context:
This painting was created during Van Gogh's voluntary confinement at the hospital in Arles, following a series of mental breakdowns. Despite his turmoil, Van Gogh produced many works during this period that reflect his surroundings and state of mind.

Symbolism and Interpretation:
The garden may symbolize a sanctuary or a place of healing, both physical and mental, during a tumultuous period in Van Gogh's life. The vibrant yet ordered garden contrasts with the chaos he was experiencing, perhaps reflecting a longing for stability and calm.

Critical Reception and Legacy:
While Van Gogh's work was not widely recognized during his lifetime, his paintings of the hospital garden are viewed as an important part of his oeuvre, offering insight into his mental state during this period. Posthumously, these works have been celebrated for their emotional depth and technical skill.

Unique or Interesting Facts:
The hospital garden series stands out in Van Gogh's work as a deeply personal reflection of his circumstances. Interestingly, Van Gogh's paintings of the hospital gardens vary in mood and color, reflecting the fluctuating nature of his mental health. Despite his struggles, these works exhibit a mastery of color and form that was ahead of its time and would go on to influence future generations of artists.

Garden of the Hospital in Saint-Rémy (1889)

Artwork Description:
The painting "Garden of the Hospital in Saint-Rémy" by Vincent van Gogh is a landscape work that captures the hospital grounds where the artist spent time as a patient. It is distinguished by its bold, swirling brushstrokes and vivid color contrasts, particularly the yellows and greens that create a sense of vitality against the somber subject matter.

Historical Context:
Van Gogh painted this scene during his stay at the Saint-Paul-de-Mausole asylum in Saint-Rémy-de-Provence in 1889. This was a period of intense productivity for Van Gogh, despite suffering from severe mental health issues. The hospital gardens provided a source of comfort and inspiration for him.

Symbolism and Interpretation:
The painting's turbulent sky and the distorted forms of the trees may reflect the inner turmoil Van Gogh was experiencing. Gardens in Van Gogh's works often symbolize shelter and respite, and the juxtaposition of the garden's beauty with the hospital setting could represent the fragile boundary between wellness and illness.

Critical Reception and Legacy:
Van Gogh's works received little recognition during his lifetime, but his posthumous fame grew rapidly in the early 20th century. Today, paintings like "Garden of the Hospital in Saint-Rémy" are celebrated for their emotive power and innovative style, which have made Van Gogh one of the most influential figures in the history of Western art.

Unique or Interesting Facts:
This painting is part of a series that Van Gogh created while at the asylum, where he was allowed to paint as part of his therapy. The series captures different views of the garden, reflecting changes in the artist's mood and the environment. Despite the challenges he faced, Van Gogh found solace in painting, which remained a therapeutic outlet for his emotional and psychological struggles.

Portrait of Patience Escalier (1888)

Artwork Description:
"Portrait of Patience Escalier" is a vibrant painting by Vincent van Gogh that depicts a local farmer from the region of Provence in France. Escalier is portrayed with a rugged, weathered face, wearing a straw hat and a blue peasant smock, against a warm, orange background. Van Gogh's use of swirling brushstrokes and bold, expressive color exemplifies his post-impressionistic style.

Historical Context:
Van Gogh painted this portrait during his period in Arles, a time when he was particularly interested in capturing the lives and characters of local peasants. Escalier was a shepherd and a gardener whose distinctive features captured Van Gogh's interest, leading to one of the most arresting portraits of his career.

Symbolism and Interpretation:
The painting can be seen as a celebration of rural life and the dignity of manual labor. Escalier's strong, worn hands and sunburnt face symbolize his hard work and connection to the land. The intense colors and bold technique may also reflect Van Gogh's desire to convey the emotional and spiritual experience of his subjects.

Critical Reception and Legacy:
Although Van Gogh was not widely recognized during his lifetime, this portrait, like many of his works, gained immense popularity posthumously. It is celebrated for its powerful depiction of character and its brilliant use of color.

Unique or Interesting Facts:
Patience Escalier was a real person whom Van Gogh got to know during his stay in Arles. The name "Patience" is quite fitting for a subject of Van Gogh, whose works often reflect themes of perseverance and endurance. Van Gogh's letters mention Escalier, providing a deeper insight into both the subject and the artist's thoughts on his work.

Gauguin's Chair (1888)

Artwork Description:
"Gauguin's Chair," by Vincent van Gogh, is an oil painting depicting Paul Gauguin's armchair, with a candle burning and a couple of books on the seat. The composition is stark and uses contrasting colors, with the green floor and red-orange chair creating a vivid scene. The background wall features a simplistic rendering of a painting within the painting, adding depth to the work.

Historical Context:
This painting was created in 1888 while Gauguin and Van Gogh were living together in the Yellow House in Arles, France. It was a time of great artistic exchange between the two, but also of personal conflict. Van Gogh painted this as part of a pair of chair paintings; the other is his own chair, representing a personal and artistic contrast between the two men.

Symbolism and Interpretation:
The empty chair is often interpreted as a portrait of Gauguin himself, with the candle symbolizing the artist's presence and the books representing knowledge or perhaps the world of ideas. The contrasting colors and the simplicity of the objects can be seen as an insight into Gauguin's character through Van Gogh's eyes.

Critical Reception and Legacy:
While Van Gogh was not commercially successful during his lifetime, his work, including "Gauguin's Chair," gained enormous posthumous recognition. This painting is particularly notable for its narrative depth, as it hints at the relationship between the two artists. It's often examined in discussions of Van Gogh's technique and his approach to symbolism in art.

Unique or Interesting Facts:
"Gauguin's Chair" serves as a counterpart to "Van Gogh's Chair," which shows a more modest, plain chair with a pipe and tobacco. The pairing of the two chairs has been interpreted as a reflection of the differences in the artists' statuses, styles, and personalities. Van Gogh's use of chairs as symbols for people was a unique approach that has intrigued art historians and critics alike.

Haystacks near a Farm (1888)

Artwork Description:
"Haystacks near a Farm," attributed to Vincent van Gogh, is a vividly colored work capturing the rustic charm of the countryside. The painting features haystacks in the foreground, with a farm scene in the background, rendered with energetic brushstrokes and a bright palette that brings a sense of life and movement to the agricultural setting.

Historical Context:
Created in 1888, this piece was painted during Van Gogh's time in Arles, a period when he was deeply inspired by the Provençal landscape. This era is marked by Van Gogh's experiments with light and color, as he sought to capture the essence of the rural countryside.

Symbolism and Interpretation:
Haystacks are a common motif in agricultural paintings and often symbolize the bounty of the harvest and the cycle of the seasons. In Van Gogh's work, they may also represent the dignity of rural labor and the beauty he found in the everyday lives of peasants and farmers.

Critical Reception and Legacy:
While Van Gogh only gained fame after his death, his paintings of rural life have become emblematic of his artistic vision and are celebrated for their vibrant color and expressive style. "Haystacks near a Farm" contributes to Van Gogh's legacy as an artist who transformed the mundane into the magnificent through his unique perspective.

Unique or Interesting Facts:
Van Gogh's interest in depicting haystacks predates the more famous series by Claude Monet, highlighting Van Gogh's role in developing this motif within the Impressionist and Post-Impressionist movements. Unlike Monet's more systematic exploration of light and time, Van Gogh's haystacks are more about color, texture, and the personal emotional response they elicit.

Houses at Auvers (1890)

Artwork Description:
"Houses at Auvers" is a painting by Vincent van Gogh that depicts a row of quaint rural homes amid a lush landscape. Characterized by Van Gogh's distinctive brushwork, the painting features a dynamic and textured sky, with the greenery and architecture rendered in bold, impasto strokes that convey depth and vibrancy.

Historical Context:
Completed in 1890 during the last few months of Van Gogh's life, this work belongs to a series of paintings he produced while living in Auvers-sur-Oise, under the care of Dr. Paul Gachet. This period was marked by intense productivity and reflection, as Van Gogh sought solace in the countryside following his time in the Saint-Rémy asylum.

Symbolism and Interpretation:
The houses, with their solid, peaceful appearance, may represent stability and shelter, contrasting with the turmoil Van Gogh experienced in his personal life. The swirling sky and vigorous application of paint could also symbolize the artist's emotional state, reflecting both chaos and beauty.

Critical Reception and Legacy:
While Van Gogh was not widely recognized in his lifetime, "Houses at Auvers" has been highly regarded by art historians and is celebrated for its poignant beauty and technical mastery. The painting reflects Van Gogh's mature style and contributes significantly to his legacy as a pioneer of modern art.

Unique or Interesting Facts:
"Houses at Auvers" captures the unique light and atmosphere of the French countryside, which had a profound impact on Van Gogh's palette and technique. This painting, along with others from the same period, marks a departure from his earlier works, as Van Gogh moved towards greater abstraction and expressive use of color and form. The Auvers series is often seen as a culmination of Van Gogh's lifelong exploration of the relationship between man and nature.

Irises (1889)

Artwork Description:
"Irises" is one of Vincent van Gogh's most celebrated works, composed of vibrant blue and purple iris flowers against a yellow background. The flowers are densely packed and seem to be in a state of natural wild growth, with one solitary white iris standing out amongst the blue.

Historical Context:
Van Gogh painted "Irises" in 1889 during his stay at the asylum in Saint-Paul-de-Mausole in Saint-Rémy-de-Provence, where he admitted himself after experiencing several episodes of acute mental distress. The irises were likely part of the asylum's garden, and the work was done a year before his death.

Symbolism and Interpretation:
The irises may represent a fleeting moment of beauty and respite from Van Gogh's mental turmoil. The white iris, different from the rest, has been interpreted as a symbol of the artist's feelings of isolation and difference. Irises, which have a rich history in art and symbolism, are often associated with hope, faith, and wisdom.

Critical Reception and Legacy:
While Van Gogh did not live to see his work celebrated, "Irises" became one of his most famous and revered pieces after his death. It reflects his intense emotional life and search for stability and tranquility. "Irises" was one of the first paintings he did while at the asylum and one of several from his prolific final period that helped solidify his reputation.

Unique or Interesting Facts:
"Irises" was one of the most expensive paintings ever sold at one time, achieving a record price at auction. Van Gogh considered it more of a study than a final work, as indicated by the lack of a signature; this was common for pieces he did not consider complete. Despite this, "Irises" stands out for its striking color contrasts and the emotional power of its brushwork, showcasing Van Gogh's masterful ability to convey emotion through the natural world.

Landscape at Sunset (1885)

Artwork Description:
"Landscape at Sunset" by Vincent van Gogh is a depiction of a tranquil rural scene as the day comes to a close. The painting features a setting sun casting a warm, golden glow over the landscape, with silhouetted trees and a figure, possibly a peasant, returning home. The sky, ablaze with yellow and orange hues, dominates the composition and contrasts with the darkening land.

Historical Context:
This piece was created during the period when Van Gogh lived in Nuenen, Netherlands, where he focused on scenes of rural life and labor. The work reflects Van Gogh's interest in the lives of peasants and the Dutch countryside, which greatly influenced his early style.

Symbolism and Interpretation:
Sunsets are often symbolic of endings or the passage of time. In the context of Van Gogh's work, this sunset might represent the conclusion of a day's labor or the cycle of nature and life. The solitary figure's presence adds a contemplative or melancholic note, perhaps reflecting the artist's own emotions.

Critical Reception and Legacy:
While Van Gogh's work received little recognition during his lifetime, his later pieces, including "Landscape at Sunset," gained significant acclaim after his death. This painting contributes to the narrative of Van Gogh as an artist who could find profound beauty in everyday scenes and is admired for its emotive use of color and light.

Unique or Interesting Facts:
Van Gogh's early works, such as "Landscape at Sunset," are distinct for their darker palette and more somber tone compared to his later, more vibrant works from the South of France. These early paintings are crucial for understanding his development as an artist and his unwavering interest in capturing the essence of rural life. This painting also exemplifies Van Gogh's transition from the influence of Dutch masters to his own unique post-impressionistic style.

Lilacs (1889)

Artwork Description:
"Lilacs" by Vincent van Gogh is a vibrant painting filled with lush lilac bushes in bloom. The foreground is dominated by the detailed lilac bush, with an explosion of white and violet flowers. The background hints at a deeper, more tranquil blue, possibly indicating water or sky, with contrasting greenery and a hint of a pathway leading through the garden.

Historical Context:
Created in 1889, Van Gogh painted "Lilacs" during his self-imposed stay at the asylum in Saint-Paul-de-Mausole in Saint-Rémy-de-Provence. This period was one of both great creativity and deep personal turmoil for Van Gogh. His works from this time often reflect the tension between his troubled psychological state and his acute sensitivity to the beauty and detail of the natural world.

Symbolism and Interpretation:
Lilacs traditionally symbolize spring and renewal, but they can also represent the fleeting nature of life, a theme that resonated with Van Gogh, particularly during his time in the asylum. The vibrancy of the flowers against the calmer background may reflect moments of clarity amidst the struggles of his mental state.

Critical Reception and Legacy:
Though Van Gogh sold only a few paintings in his lifetime and "Lilacs" may not have been well-known at the time, his work gained tremendous acclaim posthumously. "Lilacs" contributes to the appreciation of Van Gogh's work for its emotional depth and innovative brushwork, which have made him one of the most influential artists in the history of Western art.

Unique or Interesting Facts:
Van Gogh's flower paintings, including "Lilacs," were part of his exploration of color theory, which he avidly studied. His choice to use complementary colors, such as the yellows alongside the violets in this painting, was deliberate to make each color appear more vibrant. The technique of applying paint directly from the tube helped create the textured, almost three-dimensional effect seen in the lilacs' petals.

Starry Night on the Rhone (1888)

Artwork Description:
"Starry Night Over the Rhône" is a depiction of the night sky over the Rhône River in Arles, France. The painting features the bright stars and their reflections on the water's surface, with the town's gas lighting adding a warm glow to the cool blue tones of the evening.

Historical Context:
This work was painted during Van Gogh's time in Arles, a period where he was particularly focused on capturing night scenes. He was fascinated by the nocturnal effects and the challenge of portraying night on canvas.

Symbolism and Interpretation:
The painting explores themes of reflection, both literal and metaphorical, and the connection between the heavens and the earth. It reflects Van Gogh's awe of the cosmos and his attempt to capture its beauty.

Critical Reception and Legacy:
While not as famous as "The Starry Night" of 1889, this painting is highly regarded for its pioneering approach to night scenes, which were traditionally not depicted with such color and vibrancy. It showcases Van Gogh's innovative use of color and his ability to convey mood through his unique brushwork.

Unique or Interesting Facts:
Van Gogh wrote to his brother Theo about this painting, expressing his enthusiasm for painting stars. The piece is a precursor to his later work, "The Starry Night," which is one of his most famous paintings. This earlier work captures the calmness of the night sky, as opposed to the turmoil often associated with "The Starry Night."

Noon – Rest from Work (1890-91)

Artwork Description:
"Noon – Rest from Work" is a painting by Vincent van Gogh that exhibits a man and woman taking a break from the labor of harvesting. Van Gogh's use of vivid colors and bold brushstrokes imbues the scene with intensity and warmth. The contrast between the figures' relaxed poses and the vibrant, active background emphasizes the dichotomy between work and rest.

Historical Context:
Van Gogh painted this work in the final years of his life, inspired by Jean-François Millet's original. Millet was an artist Van Gogh greatly admired for his depictions of peasant life. This painting is part of a series in which Van Gogh paid homage to Millet, reinterpreting the older artist's themes with his own color and style.

Symbolism and Interpretation:
The subject of resting workers reflects Van Gogh's empathy towards the rural working class, a recurring theme in his art. The scene symbolizes the universal need for rest and the human connection to the cycles of nature. It's a celebration of everyday moments of peace and the honest, simple life of the peasantry.

Critical Reception and Legacy:
Van Gogh's reimaginations of Millet's works were initially personal exercises, not intended for exhibition. Posthumously, however, they have been recognized as significant contributions to the oeuvre of Van Gogh, showcasing his reverence for Millet and his ability to transform an existing work into something uniquely his own.

Unique or Interesting Facts:
Van Gogh's reinterpretation of Millet's work was not mere copying but rather a transformation. He used color and his own style to convey the emotional and spiritual essence he perceived in the subjects. Van Gogh often spoke of his admiration for Millet, and his reworkings serve as a clear indication of the profound influence Millet had on his artistic development.

Mulberry Tree (1889)

Artwork Description:
"The Mulberry Tree" by Vincent van Gogh is a vivid and textural painting that captures a solitary, robust mulberry tree. Its twisting branches are filled with bright yellow leaves, contrasting sharply against the bold blue sky. The painting is noted for its thick impasto strokes that give the image a dynamic sense of energy and life.

Historical Context:
Van Gogh painted "The Mulberry Tree" in 1889 while he was a patient at the Saint-Paul-de-Mausole asylum in Saint-Rémy-de-Provence. During this time, he had limited access to the outside world, yet he produced some of his most famous works, often painting the asylum's garden and the view of the surrounding countryside.

Symbolism and Interpretation:
Trees often symbolized strength and endurance to Van Gogh. The mulberry tree, with its gnarled and twisting branches, might represent resilience, especially in the face of the artist's own mental struggles. The choice of intense colors can be seen as reflective of Van Gogh's emotional state and his desire to convey the spiritual qualities he found in nature.

Critical Reception and Legacy:
While Van Gogh was not commercially successful during his lifetime, his work received critical acclaim after his death. "The Mulberry Tree" is celebrated for its bold color choices and emotive power, encapsulating Van Gogh's innovative contributions to the development of modern art.

Unique or Interesting Facts:
Van Gogh's use of color in "The Mulberry Tree" is particularly noteworthy; he often used color to express emotion, with the vibrant yellow possibly symbolizing vitality and the blue conveying depth and stability. The painting is a fine example of how Van Gogh found solace and inspiration in nature, despite his troubled circumstances. This work, like many from his time in Saint-Rémy, reflects his ongoing battle with his mental health, as well as his undiminished creative spirit.

The Old Cemetery Tower at Nuenen (1885)

Artwork Description:
The painting shows an old tower with a dilapidated appearance, surrounded by barren trees and graves marked by simple crosses. The cemetery depicted is likely the one where van Gogh's father, Theodorus, was buried. The atmosphere evokes a sense of desolation and reflects van Gogh's emotional state during this period.

Historical Context:
Van Gogh painted this scene in Nuenen, where he lived with his parents from 1883 to 1885. This was a period of productivity for van Gogh, where he focused on painting peasant life and landscapes.

Symbolism and Interpretation:
The painting can be seen as a reflection on mortality and the passage of time, themes that Van Gogh revisited throughout his work. The looming tower and overcast sky contribute to the somber mood of the piece.

Critical Reception and Legacy:
Like many of van Gogh's works, this painting was not recognized during his lifetime but has since become appreciated for its emotional depth and beauty. It is a testament to van Gogh's ability to transform a simple scene into a poignant work of art.

Unique or Interesting Facts:
This painting is significant as it captures a personal moment for van Gogh, being the resting place of his father. It also demonstrates van Gogh's early style, characterized by dark colors and a focus on the hardships of rural life, before he developed his more vibrant, later style.

Technical Aspects:
Van Gogh's use of earthy tones and the thick application of paint is evident in this work, creating a textured surface that adds to the overall sense of decay and the passage of time depicted in the scene.

Oleanders (1888)

Artwork Description:
"Oleanders" by Vincent van Gogh is a still life painting that exudes vibrancy through its depiction of pink oleander blossoms in a simple earthenware jug. Set against a stark lime-green background, the lush, flowering oleanders are accompanied by Van Gogh's choice of literature, with a yellow book prominently placed on the table, adding a layer of intellectual depth to the composition.

Historical Context:
Van Gogh created "Oleanders" in 1888 while living in Arles, France, a period when he was deeply inspired by the light and color of the Provence region. This painting reflects his continuous exploration of the still life genre and his fascination with the symbolic and expressive potential of flowers.

Symbolism and Interpretation:
Oleanders are known for their beauty as well as their poisonous qualities, a dichotomy that might have appealed to Van Gogh's sense of beauty tinged with danger or sorrow. The flowers can be interpreted as a metaphor for life's dual nature — its capacity for beauty and peril. The presence of the book suggests the comfort and escape that intellectual and artistic pursuits provided to Van Gogh.

Critical Reception and Legacy:
While Van Gogh did not receive much recognition during his lifetime, "Oleanders" now stands among his more acclaimed works, appreciated for its vivid color palette and emotional resonance. It exemplifies his ability to infuse ordinary subjects with intense significance and beauty.

Unique or Interesting Facts:
Van Gogh often used floral still lifes to express his feelings and worked on "Oleanders" at a time of great artistic innovation and personal hope. The book in the painting is by Émile Zola, whose work Van Gogh admired for its social realism and its focus on the lives of ordinary people, reflecting Van Gogh's own artistic inclinations. The use of complementary colors — the pinks and greens — showcases Van Gogh's evolving color theories and his departure from the darker palette of his earlier Dutch period.

Peasant Woman Against a Background of Wheat (1890)

Artwork Description:
"Peasant Woman Against a Background of Wheat" by Vincent van Gogh is a striking portrait of a rural woman. The subject is rendered with coarse features and a sturdy build, typical of Van Gogh's depictions of peasant figures. Her attire is simple, and she is set against a vibrant background of golden wheat, with bold, expressive brushstrokes that emphasize the textures of the natural world around her.

Historical Context:
Created in 1890, during the final year of Van Gogh's life, this painting reflects his continued interest in the lives of peasants and agricultural workers, a theme he explored throughout his career. Van Gogh's move to Auvers-sur-Oise, where this painting was likely created, provided him with new rural subjects for his work at a time when he was grappling with severe mental health issues.

Symbolism and Interpretation:
Van Gogh often used his art to convey a sense of solidarity with the working class. The robust figure of the peasant woman symbolizes the dignity of labor and the connection between humans and the land. The wheat may represent sustenance and the cycle of growth and harvest, themes resonant with Van Gogh's fascination with nature and the human condition.

Critical Reception and Legacy:
While not widely known during his lifetime, Van Gogh's depictions of peasant life have come to be celebrated for their empathetic portrayal of his subjects. "Peasant Woman Against a Background of Wheat" contributes to the narrative of Van Gogh as a compassionate observer of human life and an artist who could communicate profound truths through his work.

Unique or Interesting Facts:
Van Gogh's peasant portraits are heavily influenced by Jean-François Millet, a Barbizon School painter whom Van Gogh admired for his depictions of rural laborers. Van Gogh sought to capture the essence of his subjects through color and gesture, often choosing colors that would enhance the emotional impact of the image rather than striving for realistic representation. This portrait, like many of Van Gogh's works, is noted for its emotional intensity, conveyed through a vibrant palette and dynamic brushwork.

Pine Trees at Sunset (1889)

Artwork Description:
"Pine Trees at Sunset" by Vincent van Gogh is a work that captures the dramatic effect of the setting sun on a landscape dominated by tall pine trees. The female figure, small and cloaked, moves through the scene, adding a sense of scale and solitude. Van Gogh's swirling brushstrokes create a sense of movement in the sky, contrasting with the solid, dark forms of the trees.

Historical Context:
Painted in 1889, this piece likely originates from Van Gogh's period at the Saint-Paul asylum in Saint-Rémy-de-Provence. This was a highly productive phase for Van Gogh, where he painted many of his most renowned pieces. The subjects often included the asylum's surroundings and were infused with emotional significance.

Symbolism and Interpretation:
The depiction of the sunset may symbolize the end of a cycle or day, possibly reflecting Van Gogh's contemplation of his own life and career, which was filled with personal challenges. The solitary figure might represent loneliness or introspection, common themes in Van Gogh's work.

Critical Reception and Legacy:
Van Gogh's works, including this painting, were not widely recognized during his lifetime but have since gained immense critical acclaim. His style has influenced generations of artists, and his pieces are studied for their emotional depth and innovative technique.

Unique or Interesting Facts:
Van Gogh was known for painting "en plein air" (outdoors), capturing his immediate impressions of the scene. His expressive use of color and form in this painting is a good example of how he could convey mood and atmosphere. The presence of a human figure in his landscape paintings is relatively rare, making this work particularly intriguing as it invites viewers to ponder the story behind the solitary wanderer.

Portrait of Armand Roulin (1888)

Artwork Description:
"Portrait of Armand Roulin" is one of several portraits that Vincent van Gogh painted of the Roulin family. In this work, Armand is depicted in a vibrant yellow jacket, with a blue hat and a black tie, which strikingly contrast with the bold, flat green background. Van Gogh's signature expressive brushstrokes give texture to Armand's face, highlighting his youthful features and introspective gaze.

Historical Context:
In 1888, Van Gogh was living in Arles, where he became friends with the Roulin family. Postman Joseph Roulin, Armand's father, became one of Van Gogh's favorite subjects, and he painted various members of the family on multiple occasions. These portraits are among the most celebrated of Van Gogh's works from his Arles period.

Symbolism and Interpretation:
The bright colors and forthright presentation in "Portrait of Armand Roulin" may reflect Van Gogh's view of Armand as a modern and forward-thinking young man. The choice of colors can also be seen as Van Gogh's continued experimentation with color theory, using complementary colors to create a sense of vibrancy and depth.

Critical Reception and Legacy:
While Van Gogh's works were not commercially successful during his lifetime, his portraits of the Roulin family have become some of his most valued pieces. They are often noted for their emotional depth and for the unique way in which they capture the essence of the sitters.

Unique or Interesting Facts:
Van Gogh's relationship with the Roulin family was one of mutual affection and respect. The postman, Joseph Roulin, was a supportive friend to Van Gogh during his time in Arles, and this close bond is evident in the care and attention Van Gogh took in painting his family's portraits. Van Gogh's letters often mention the Roulins, indicating the significant place they held in his life.

Fishing Boats on the Beach at Saintes-Maries-de-la-Mer (1888)

Artwork Description:
"Fishing Boats on the Beach at Saintes-Maries-de-la-Mer" is a vibrant work capturing the seaside ambience with a series of boats grounded on the shore. Van Gogh's use of bright colors and dynamic brushstrokes vividly conveys the light and atmosphere of the Mediterranean setting.

Historical Context:
Van Gogh painted this scene during his stay in Arles, in the south of France, where he was inspired by the landscape and the fishing community of Saintes-Maries-de-la-Mer. This period was marked by a prolific output of paintings reflecting the luminous quality of the region's light.

Symbolism and Interpretation:
While less symbolic than some of his other work, the choice of fishing boats may reflect Van Gogh's fascination with the livelihoods of ordinary people and his desire to capture the essence of their daily lives. The depiction of boats on land may also allude to themes of rest or transition.

Critical Reception and Legacy:
While Van Gogh's work was not widely acclaimed during his lifetime, his paintings of Saintes-Maries-de-la-Mer are now celebrated for their bold application of color and innovative composition. They have contributed to Van Gogh's posthumous fame and are seen as pivotal in his artistic journey towards greater abstraction and expressionism.

Unique or Interesting Facts:
Van Gogh wrote to his brother Theo about this painting, expressing his enthusiasm for the marine subject and the challenge of capturing the movement and color of the sea. He also created several drawings and paintings of the scene, experimenting with different perspectives and techniques, demonstrating his intense study of the subject.

Portrait of Trabuc (1889)

Artwork Description:
The painting features François Trabuc, the chief orderly at the Saint-Paul-de-Mausole asylum in Saint-Rémy-de-Provence, where Van Gogh stayed after his infamous ear-cutting incident. Van Gogh's portrait of Trabuc is striking for its intense scrutiny of the sitter's character. Trabuc is depicted with a stern, contemplative expression, wearing a striped garment that is rendered with Van Gogh's characteristic swirling brushstrokes.

Historical Context:
This work was created during Van Gogh's voluntary confinement at the Saint-Paul-de-Mausole asylum. The period was one of great productivity for Van Gogh, who found the subjects for his paintings in the environment and people around the asylum.

Symbolism and Interpretation:
The portrait may reflect Van Gogh's thoughts on authority and discipline, as Trabuc was an authority figure in the asylum. The choice of a subdued palette and the direct gaze might suggest Van Gogh's attempt to capture Trabuc's inner strength and the solemnity of his position.

Critical Reception and Legacy:
Although Van Gogh sold only a few paintings in his lifetime, his portraits, including this one, have been highly praised for their emotional depth and innovative use of color and technique. The painting of Trabuc is no exception and is admired for its psychological penetration.

Unique or Interesting Facts:
Trabuc was known for his strict demeanor, which is thought to be captured in the portrait. Van Gogh had a particular interest in portraying the staff and patients of the asylum, as they were his primary human subjects during his stay. This painting is part of a series of portraits that provide a window into the world of the asylum and Van Gogh's state of mind during that period.

Terrace in the Luxembourg Gardens (1886)

Artwork Description:
This work depicts the Luxembourg Gardens in Paris, a place Van Gogh would frequent. The scene captures the leisurely ambiance of Parisian life, with figures strolling and sitting amongst the greenery of the gardens.

Historical Context:
The Luxembourg Gardens were a popular subject for many artists of the time. This painting was created during Van Gogh's stay in Paris, where he was exposed to new artistic movements like Impressionism and Pointillism, which influenced his use of color and light.

Symbolism and Interpretation:
Van Gogh's work often reflects his emotional and psychological state. While this painting may not be as emotionally charged as his later works, it shows his transition towards brighter, more varied colors and a lighter mood compared to his earlier, darker Dutch works.

Critical Reception and Legacy:
Van Gogh's Parisian paintings are not as well-known as his later works from Arles, Saint-Rémy, and Auvers. However, they were crucial to his development as an artist, marking a period of experimentation and growth.

Unique or Interesting Facts:
The Luxembourg Gardens were created in the early 17th century by Marie de' Medici. By Van Gogh's time, they had become a hub of Parisian social life, encapsulating the modernity and dynamism that would come to characterize Paris in the late 19th century. Van Gogh's depiction of the gardens is less about the accuracy of the place and more about capturing the interplay of light, color, and movement.

Prisoners Exercising (1890)

Artwork Description:
This piece, also known as "Prisoners' Round", depicts prisoners walking in a circle in a prison yard, watched by guards. The scene is based on an engraving by Gustave Doré. Van Gogh's version is characterized by his typical thick brushstrokes and his use of color to convey the dreary atmosphere of the prison.

Historical Context:
Van Gogh painted this during his stay at the Saint-Paul-de-Mausole asylum in Saint-Rémy-de-Provence. During this time, his work reflected his psychological state and the themes of isolation and despair, as seen in the repetitive, circular motion of the prisoners which can be seen as a metaphor for his own feelings of being trapped.

Symbolism and Interpretation:
The circular movement of the prisoners may symbolize the monotonous and unending nature of prison life, as well as the mental state of someone trapped in their own cycle of thoughts. The figure standing in the foreground, who is illuminated and facing a different direction, could represent the artist's self-portrait and his desire to break free from this cycle.

Critical Reception and Legacy:
While not widely known during Van Gogh's lifetime, "Prisoners Exercising" has been recognized for its intense emotion and poignant commentary on the human condition. It is a powerful example of Van Gogh's ability to empathize with the suffering of others and his use of art to express complex emotional and psychological states.

Unique or Interesting Facts:
"Prisoners Exercising" is a reflection of Van Gogh's interest in the work of Charles Dickens and Victor Hugo, who both wrote about social injustice and the lives of the poor and marginalized, including prisoners. The painting also shows Van Gogh's respect for Doré, whose works he admired for their social commentary.

Self-Portrait as a Painter (1887-88)

Artwork Description:
In this self-portrait, Vincent van Gogh portrays himself as an artist, with the tools of his trade—palette, brushes, and canvas—clearly visible. The focus on his intense gaze and the vivid colors reflect his dedication to art.

Historical Context:
Van Gogh painted this during his time in Paris, a period of profound artistic development influenced by Impressionism and Japanese prints. It was a time when he experimented with lighter colors and new brushwork techniques.

Symbolism and Interpretation:
The portrait symbolizes van Gogh's identity as an artist. It's a statement of self-affirmation in his chosen profession. The paint on the palette and the unfinished canvas signify the ongoing work and creativity of his life.

Critical Reception and Legacy:
Van Gogh was not famous during his lifetime, but his self-portraits have become some of the most iconic images in art history. This painting contributes to our understanding of his self-perception as an artist and his relentless passion for painting.

Unique or Interesting Facts:
This work is one of many self-portraits by Van Gogh, in which he often explored his identity and emotional state. Unlike other artists of his time, van Gogh often used himself as a subject, offering a deep psychological insight into his world.

The Sower at Sunset (1888)

Artwork Description:
This composition features a sower working in the field at sunset. The large, setting sun dominates the background, casting a warm yellow glow that contrasts with the cool blue of the field. The sower's figure is in silhouette, reinforcing the theme of man's connection to the land.

Historical Context:
Van Gogh painted several versions of The Sower, which was inspired by Jean-François Millet's work, a painter Van Gogh greatly admired. This painting reflects Van Gogh's interest in the cycles of nature and the dignity of labor, common themes in his work while he was in Arles, France.

Symbolism and Interpretation:
The sower is a symbol of fertility and renewal, which is a recurring motif in art history. Van Gogh often associated the act of sowing with his own work as an artist, spreading ideas and beauty through his paintings.

Critical Reception and Legacy:
Van Gogh's sower paintings have been widely studied for their innovative use of color and for their emotional depth. The work is seen as an expression of Van Gogh's connection to the earth and the common man.

Unique or Interesting Facts:
The Sower at Sunset is notable for its vibrant color contrasts, which were part of Van Gogh's exploration of complementary colors. The painting also captures the transitional moment of dusk, a time that Van Gogh considered to be full of poetic potential.

The Cottage (1885)

Artwork Description:
This painting depicts a rural cottage at dusk, with a figure standing at the entrance. The scene is imbued with a sense of tranquility and simplicity, characteristic of Van Gogh's work during his Nuenen period, where he focused on peasant life and landscapes.

Historical Context:
During this time, Van Gogh was living in the Netherlands and was profoundly influenced by the lives of local peasants and farmers. His work from this period sought to depict the reality of rural life, often with an emphasis on the harshness and labor of their existence.

Symbolism and Interpretation:
The cottage as a subject can be seen as a symbol of the simple, unadorned life of the rural poor. The twilight setting may reflect the end of the day's labor and the harshness of life. This painting, with its somber tones and mood, reflects Van Gogh's empathy for the struggles of the peasant class.

Critical Reception and Legacy:
While Van Gogh's earlier work was not widely known or appreciated during his lifetime, his portrayal of peasant life contributed to the development of his style and his exploration of color and form. These themes would become central to his later, more celebrated works.

Unique or Interesting Facts:
Van Gogh's focus on such subjects was partly inspired by the works of Jean-François Millet, a French painter who was also known for his depictions of peasant life. "The Cottage" reflects Van Gogh's commitment to representing the laboring class with dignity and depth.

The Large Plane Trees (1889)

Artwork Description:
This work captures a road in Saint-Rémy-de-Provence lined with plane trees, creating a bold and dynamic depiction of the landscape. The thick brushstrokes and vibrant colors are typical of Van Gogh's style during his time at the asylum in Saint-Rémy, where he produced some of his most famous works.

Historical Context:
Van Gogh painted this scene during his voluntary stay at the Saint-Paul-de-Mausole asylum. Despite his mental health struggles, he was prolific during this period, often painting the clinic's gardens or views from its windows.

Symbolism and Interpretation:
The plane trees might symbolize resilience and endurance, as these trees are known for their longevity and strength. The intense colors and swirling patterns could reflect Van Gogh's turbulent emotional state at the time of painting.

Critical Reception and Legacy:
While not as widely recognized as some of his other works from the same period, "The Large Plane Trees" is celebrated for its innovative use of color and form, which influenced the development of Expressionism. Van Gogh's paintings from this time are considered some of the most important works in Western art history.

Unique or Interesting Facts:
Van Gogh created this painting as part of a series while he was experimenting with reproducing the effects of Japanese woodcuts, which he greatly admired. The bold outlines and flat areas of color are indicative of this influence. Additionally, he often chose to paint en plein air (outdoors) to directly capture the effects of light and color in nature, even while confined to the grounds of the asylum.

Self-Portrait with a Straw Hat (1887-88)

Artwork Description:
This self-portrait features Van Gogh in a straw hat, with a neutral expression. The use of light and vibrant brushstrokes is typical of his work during his Paris period, showing the influence of Impressionism and pointillism.

Historical Context:
During the time Van Gogh painted this self-portrait, he was living in Paris and was deeply immersed in refining his technique and experimenting with the bright palette of the Impressionists and the pointillist technique.

Symbolism and Interpretation:
Van Gogh's choice of a straw hat, typically worn by peasants, may reflect his identification with the working class and his respect for manual labor. The intense gaze may symbolize the artist's search for personal and artistic identity.

Critical Reception and Legacy:
While Van Gogh was not commercially successful during his lifetime, his self-portraits have since become some of the most recognizable and celebrated works in art history, deeply appreciated for their emotional depth and innovative style.

Unique or Interesting Facts:
Van Gogh's self-portraits are notable for their raw introspection. This particular self-portrait is interesting because it demonstrates Van Gogh's practice of painting on both sides of the canvas; the reverse side features "The Potato Peeler." This was likely due to the financial constraints he often faced.

Edge of a Wood (1882)

Artwork Description
The painting depicts a dense forest scene, rich with dark tones and subtle light filtering through the trees. Van Gogh captures the tranquility and mystery of the forest edge using muted colors and loose brushstrokes.

Historical Context
Created during van Gogh's early period when he was living in The Hague, this work reflects the influence of the Dutch landscape and the Barbizon school, which emphasized the beauty of the natural world and influenced van Gogh's early style.

Symbolism and Interpretation
Forests often symbolize the unknown or the subconscious in art. In Edge of a Wood, van Gogh may be exploring themes of solitude, reflection, or the contrasting forces of light and darkness.

Critical Reception and Legacy
Van Gogh's early works received little attention during his lifetime, but they are now appreciated for their contribution to his development as an artist. This painting is an example of his experimentation with light and shadow, which would become more pronounced in his later works.

Unique or Interesting Facts
Van Gogh's early period is marked by a more restrained color palette and traditional subjects compared to his later, more vibrant works. This painting exemplifies his exploration of natural scenes before his move to France, where his style evolved significantly.

Technical Aspects
In Edge of a Wood, van Gogh uses a variety of brushstrokes to create texture, with thicker paint in the foreground and thinner, more fluid strokes to depict the light behind the trees. The composition leads the viewer's eye into the depth of the forest, using the trees as natural lines.

The Night Café (1888)

Artwork Description:
"The Night Café" depicts the interior of the Café de la Gare in Arles, France. Van Gogh's use of contrasting colors and perspectives creates a sense of disquiet and unease. The composition includes a billiards table in the foreground, patrons at tables in the background, and a solitary figure of the proprietor. The vibrant colors and swirling ceiling and floors contribute to the painting's emotional intensity.

Historical Context:
Van Gogh created this painting during his time in Arles, a period where he was prolific but also struggled with severe mental health issues. He aimed to express the atmosphere of the café, which he described as a place where one could ruin oneself, go mad, or commit a crime.

Symbolism and Interpretation:
The vivid colors and exaggerated forms in "The Night Café" are interpreted as representations of the sordidness and depravity Van Gogh perceived in the nightlife establishment. The garish lighting and distorted spatial perspective add to the sense of an oppressive, unsettling environment, perhaps reflecting Van Gogh's own inner turmoil.

Critical Reception and Legacy:
Initially, the painting was not well-received, as its bold colors and rough style were unconventional. Over time, however, it has become one of Van Gogh's most famous works, recognized for its emotional depth and innovative technique. It is often discussed in studies of color theory and expressionism in art.

Unique or Interesting Facts:
Van Gogh stayed up for three consecutive nights to paint "The Night Café," sleeping during the day. He wanted to capture the "terrible passions of humanity" by using colors that he associated with "the red blood and the green bile." This work is also noted for its influence on later artists, including the Expressionists and Fauvists, who drew inspiration from Van Gogh's expressive use of color and brushwork.

The Painter on his Way to Work (1888)

Artwork Description:
"The Painter on the Way to Work" by Vincent van Gogh depicts a figure, likely an artist given the title, walking through a sun-drenched landscape, presumably on the way to a location of labor or inspiration. The figure carries what appears to be painting equipment, and the work is characterized by bold, expressive brushstrokes and a vivid color palette typical of Van Gogh's style.

Historical Context:
The painting was created during Van Gogh's time in Arles, France, a period when he produced some of his most renowned works. 1888 was a prolific year for Van Gogh, filled with experiments in color and technique. His time in Arles was significant for his development as an artist.

Symbolism and Interpretation:
The lone figure can be seen as a symbol of the artist's journey, both literally and metaphorically. The path represents the artist's search for creative expression and the solitude of the creative process. The bright, unforgiving light of the sun may symbolize the clarity of vision and purpose the artist seeks.

Critical Reception and Legacy:
While Van Gogh was not widely recognized during his lifetime, his work later received critical acclaim for its emotional depth and innovative use of color and brushwork. This painting contributes to the narrative of Van Gogh's dedication to his craft, despite his struggles with mental health.

Unique or Interesting Facts:
Unfortunately, the original painting was destroyed during World War II. It's known only through black and white photographs and written descriptions, making it a lost piece of Van Gogh's oeuvre and adding a layer of mystique to its legacy. The painting's loss emphasizes the fragility of cultural heritage during times of conflict.

Peach Tree in Blossom (1888)

Artwork Description:
"Peach Tree in Blossom" is a vibrant work by Vincent van Gogh that captures the delicate beauty of a peach tree during spring. Characterized by his signature expressive brushwork, the painting is rich in color, with pink blossoms set against a backdrop of a clear blue sky. The composition creates a sense of depth and vitality, emphasizing the tree's natural elegance.

Historical Context:
This painting was created in 1888 while Van Gogh was living in Arles, in the South of France. It was part of his exploration of the blossoming orchards in the region, a subject that he found deeply inspiring. The series of orchard paintings marked a period of great productivity and high spirits for Van Gogh.

Symbolism and Interpretation:
For Van Gogh, blooming orchards were symbolic of new life and hope, themes that were central to his work and personal aspirations. The peach tree in bloom, with its transient beauty, may also reflect the fleeting nature of life, a poignant theme considering Van Gogh's own struggles.

Critical Reception and Legacy:
Van Gogh's orchard series, including "Peach Tree in Blossom," has been celebrated for its vibrant use of color and evocative depiction of the countryside. While recognition of his genius largely came after his death, Van Gogh's paintings have since become some of the most famous and beloved works in the history of art.

Unique or Interesting Facts:
Van Gogh wrote to his brother Theo about the orchard series, expressing his enthusiasm for the subject matter. He often worked on several canvases at once, capturing different trees in various stages of bloom. "Peach Tree in Blossom" is especially noted for its optimistic tone and is considered one of the finest examples of Van Gogh's work from his period in Arles. This time was one of the most harmonious and artistically innovative periods of his life, despite the mental health challenges he faced.

The Potato Eaters (1885)

Artwork Description:
The painting is rendered in somber earth tones and illustrates five figures around a table eating potatoes and drinking coffee. The use of light and shadow is dramatic, with the lamp casting a glow that highlights their hands and faces, underscoring the central role of their meal and fellowship.

Historical Context:
Van Gogh painted "The Potato Eaters" while living in Nuenen, Netherlands. This period was marked by his interest in capturing the lives of the working class. It was an attempt to portray the harsh reality of country life, hence the dark colors and coarse features of the subjects.

Symbolism and Interpretation:
Van Gogh intended this painting to show the reality of peasant life, hence the lack of beautification or idealization of his subjects. The painting is often seen as a symbol of rural authenticity and laborious life. The dim lighting and coarse hands of the figures symbolize their hard work and connection to the land.

Critical Reception and Legacy:
The painting was not well-received initially, criticized for its dark palette and rough technique. However, it has since become one of Van Gogh's most famous works, often cited for its honest depiction of peasant life. It is an important work in Van Gogh's oeuvre, as it represents his early foray into the expressive potential of color and form that would become his signature in later years.

Unique or Interesting Facts:
Van Gogh considered "The Potato Eaters" to be one of his most successful works of his early period. He wanted the painting to depict the peasants as they really were, so he chose not to beautify them, which was against the conventions of the art of his time. He aimed to show that they had 'earned their food by working for it'. It's also notable for being one of the few group portraits he ever painted.

The Reaper (1889)

Artwork Description:
The painting shows a solitary figure bent over the task of reaping wheat in a field. The reaper is engulfed in the golden hues of the crop, with a vibrant blue sky above that has the characteristic swirling pattern. The use of color is striking, with the blue of the reaper's clothing providing a stark contrast to the yellow of the wheat, a color scheme Van Gogh often used to express his intense feelings.

Historical Context:
This painting reflects Van Gogh's fascination with the agrarian lifestyle and his romanticized view of peasants working the land. It was during this period that Van Gogh was producing some of his most profound work, despite the tumultuous state of his mental health.

Symbolism and Interpretation:
The reaper is often seen as a symbol of the cycle of life and death, a theme that preoccupied Van Gogh. The act of reaping can be interpreted as a metaphor for the finality of death but also the sustenance of life through the harvest. Van Gogh's own letters express a connection between the reaper and death, but not in a morose sense; instead, he saw it as a serene, almost peaceful inevitability.

Critical Reception and Legacy:
While Van Gogh did not live to see his art gain the fame it has today, his posthumous reputation has grown immensely. "The Reaper" adds to the narrative of Van Gogh as an artist who could find beauty in the everyday life of peasants and laborers, which has resonated with art lovers worldwide.

Unique or Interesting Facts:
Van Gogh's interest in depicting the reaper can be traced back to his admiration for Jean-François Millet, a French painter who also focused on peasant subjects. However, Van Gogh's interpretation is uniquely his own, filled with motion and emotion, a departure from Millet's more static and somber representations. This painting also showcases Van Gogh's innovative technique of applying paint thickly, known as impasto, which gives the work a three-dimensional quality.

Wheat Field with Cypresses (1889)

Artwork Description:
"Wheat Field with Cypresses" is characterized by a dynamic sky, swirling clouds, and the richly textured wheat field. The towering cypresses stand prominently against the tumultuous sky, anchoring the composition. The painting is infused with a sense of movement through van Gogh's signature brushstrokes.

Historical Context:
This painting was created during van Gogh's time at the Saint-Rémy asylum. Despite his troubled circumstances, this period was one of extraordinary productivity for van Gogh, and the painting reflects his sustained interest in the symbolic and expressive potential of the landscape.

Symbolism and Interpretation:
Cypresses were a subject of particular significance to van Gogh, symbolizing death and eternity due to their use in French cemeteries. However, in this painting, they also seem to represent a bridge between life and the heavens above, echoing van Gogh's ongoing quest for solace and stability in nature.

Critical Reception and Legacy:
While van Gogh was not widely recognized during his lifetime, his posthumous fame grew quickly after his death. "Wheat Field with Cypresses" is now considered one of his masterpieces and a quintessential example of his unique style and emotional depth.

Unique or Interesting Facts:
Van Gogh created several versions of this scene. The painting is notable for its use of the impasto technique, where paint is laid on an area of the surface in very thick layers. Also, van Gogh referred to this painting in his letters as one of his best summer landscapes.

The Red Vineyard at Arles (1888)

Artwork Description:
The painting shows laborers harvesting in a vineyard, with a vivid array of colors, especially the reds and oranges of the vines, which stand out against the complementary greens and blues of the landscape. The sun hangs large in the sky, casting a bright yellow glow that reflects off the river in the background.

Historical Context:
Van Gogh painted this scene in early November 1888, shortly after his move to Arles in the South of France, a period where he was particularly prolific. This was a time of intense work and creativity for Van Gogh, who was inspired by the light and landscape of the region.

Symbolism and Interpretation:
The painting can be seen as a celebration of rural labor and the beauty of the harvest. The rich, warm colors may symbolize the intense and passionate connection that Van Gogh felt to nature and the countryside. The use of a bright yellow sun also reflects Van Gogh's fascination with the effects of light.

Critical Reception and Legacy:
While Van Gogh was not commercially successful during his lifetime, this painting stands out as a landmark in his career for being sold. Today, it is celebrated for its bold color and emotive representation of the landscape and is considered one of Van Gogh's most significant works.

Unique or Interesting Facts:
The painting was bought by the Belgian artist Anna Boch during the exhibition "Les XX" in 1890 for 400 francs. Interestingly, the reality of this being the only painting Van Gogh sold is often debated; however, it remains a widely accepted part of the Van Gogh lore. The painting's location in the Pushkin Museum in Moscow makes it one of the few Van Gogh paintings to reside in a public collection in Russia.

The Starry Night (1889)

Artwork Description:
"The Starry Night" is a vibrant and emotive portrayal of the night sky, with swirling blues and yellows, a quiet town below, and a tumultuous cypress tree in the foreground. Its brushwork is bold and dynamic, creating a sense of movement and energy.

Historical Context:
Van Gogh painted this masterpiece during his stay at the Saint-Paul-de-Mausole asylum in Saint-Rémy-de-Provence, France. Despite his troubled mental state, he produced this work from memory during the day while reflecting on the night sky.

Symbolism and Interpretation:
The painting is often interpreted as reflecting Van Gogh's inner turmoil and mental health struggles. The cypress tree, traditionally associated with mourning, might represent death or the afterlife. The stars and swirling sky have been interpreted as Van Gogh's contemplation of eternity and nature's beauty.

Critical Reception and Legacy:
While "The Starry Night" was not well-received during Van Gogh's lifetime, it has since become one of the most recognized and admired paintings in art history. It is a quintessential example of expressionism in art, where emotion and personal response to the world take precedence over realistic representation.

Unique or Interesting Facts:
Interestingly, Van Gogh considered "The Starry Night" among his less successful works. The painting's fame grew posthumously, resonating with a wide audience for its emotional depth and stunning beauty. It has inspired countless works of art, literature, and music and holds a prominent place in modern culture.

Self-Portrait (1887)

Artwork Description:
This self-portrait features Van Gogh himself, with a keen and intense gaze, looking off to the side. He is depicted with his iconic red beard and hair, wearing a dark brown suit. The background consists of a rich, pointillistic texture of blues and greens, which contrast sharply with the warmer tones of his face and beard.

Historical Context:
Van Gogh painted this self-portrait during his time in Paris, a period when he was exposed to the works of the Impressionists and Neo-Impressionists. This painting reflects the influence of Pointillism, a technique that involves painting small, distinct dots of color in patterns to form an image.

Symbolism and Interpretation:
Self-portraits were a significant part of Van Gogh's oeuvre, allowing him to experiment with color, technique, and expression. This painting is a testament to his evolving style and his exploration of identity and emotional states through art.

Critical Reception and Legacy:
Van Gogh's self-portraits are among the most celebrated in art history for their raw emotional depth and innovative use of color and brushwork. They offer a window into the artist's soul and have been extensively studied and admired.

Unique or Interesting Facts:
Van Gogh created over thirty-five self-portraits during his lifetime, which was relatively short but prolific. He often used himself as a model due to lack of funds to pay for models and a desire to practice portrait painting.

Fishing Boats at Sea (1888)

Artwork Description:
"Fishing Boats at Sea," painted by Vincent van Gogh in 1888, showcases a group of boats with their sails unfurled on the sunlit, churning waters near Saintes-Maries-de-la-Mer. The energetic strokes and bold blue hues capture the sea's movement and reflect Van Gogh's fascination with the marine landscape.

Historical Context:
This work was created during Van Gogh's time in Arles, a period where the artist was particularly taken with the Provençal landscape and sought to capture its distinct light and vibrant colors. His stay in Arles was one of the most productive and innovative periods of his career.

Symbolism and Interpretation:
While Van Gogh's work is often devoid of overt symbolism, the dynamic depiction of the sea can be interpreted as a mirror of his emotional state, with the tumultuous waves reflecting the turmoil he experienced. Additionally, the fishermen's laborious life at sea might symbolize the human struggle against the forces of nature.

Critical Reception and Legacy:
Van Gogh's paintings of Saintes-Maries-de-la-Mer were not widely recognized during his lifetime, but they have since been acknowledged as significant contributions to the Post-Impressionist movement. His expressive use of color and form in this painting has been influential in the development of modern art.

Unique or Interesting Facts:
Van Gogh was known to be captivated by the Mediterranean Sea, and this painting is one of several where he experimented with different techniques to capture the essence of water and the reflections of light. What is particularly notable about this painting is Van Gogh's departure from the more traditional, smooth representations of water to a more textured, vibrant style that communicates the water's motion and the atmosphere of the seaside.

The White Orchard (1888)

Artwork Description:
This painting features a blooming orchard with white blossoms, showcasing van Gogh's unique style of vibrant colors and bold brushstrokes. The trees are foregrounded against a blue sky, with the ground covered in green and blue shades, indicating the fresh growth of spring.

Historical Context:
Van Gogh painted "The White Orchard" and other orchard paintings during his time in Arles, France, in the spring of 1888. This period was one of the most prolific and significant in van Gogh's life, where he sought to capture the essence of the countryside and the changing seasons.

Symbolism and Interpretation:
Orchards in bloom were a recurring theme for van Gogh, symbolizing awakening and renewal. The portrayal of the orchard with its blossoming trees can be seen as a metaphor for hope and the cycle of life.

Critical Reception and Legacy:
While van Gogh's work was not widely recognized during his lifetime, his orchard paintings, including "The White Orchard," are now celebrated for their innovative use of color and brushwork. These works played a significant role in the foundation of modern art and continue to influence artists today.

Unique or Interesting Facts:
Van Gogh's interest in Japanese art is reflected in the composition and the flat application of color in this painting, displaying his adaptation of Japanese woodblock print aesthetics into his work. This painting, like many of his others, reflects his ambition to bring out the intensity of color and emotion through his depiction of nature.

The Yellow House (1888)

Artwork Description:
This work depicts the house in Arles, France, where Van Gogh rented four rooms. This "Yellow House" was meant to be a haven for artists, and Van Gogh famously lived there with Paul Gauguin for a time. The vibrant yellow facade of the building stands out against the deep blue of the night sky, and the scene is rendered with the energetic brushstrokes characteristic of Van Gogh's style.

Historical Context:
Van Gogh moved to Arles in search of the bright light and vivid colors of the Provençal landscape. The Yellow House became an important subject for him, representing both the comfort of home and his aspirations for a collaborative artistic community.

Symbolism and Interpretation:
The use of contrasting colors - the yellow of the house against the blue of the sky - is typical of Van Gogh's expressive use of color to convey emotions. The Yellow House symbolizes Van Gogh's hope for a utopian artist's colony, and the empty street can be seen as indicative of his isolation.

Critical Reception and Legacy:
While Van Gogh did not achieve fame during his lifetime, his posthumous recognition has made works like "The Yellow House" highly celebrated. The painting is admired for its bold color choices and its insight into Van Gogh's life and ambitions.

Unique or Interesting Facts:
"The Yellow House" is also significant because it was here that Van Gogh's mental health began to deteriorate, leading to the infamous ear-cutting incident and his subsequent hospitalization. The house was damaged during World War II and later demolished, making the painting an important historical document of what the place looked like during Van Gogh's time.

The Zouave (1888)

Artwork Description:
The portrait features a half-length figure of a Zouave soldier, identifiable by his distinctive uniform, including a red fez and yellow accented decorative jacket. The soldier's pose is relaxed, yet his gaze is direct, conveying a sense of individual personality. The background is a vibrant green, contrasting sharply with the red of the fez and the rich blue of the soldier's vest.

Historical Context:
Van Gogh was fascinated by the colorful uniforms of the Zouaves, Algerian light infantry troops serving in the French army. During his time in Arles, Van Gogh painted a series of portraits featuring a Zouave, which allowed him to experiment with color and expression.

Symbolism and Interpretation:
The Zouave's uniform in the painting is not merely a depiction of military attire but a canvas for Van Gogh's exploration of color theory. He used complementary colors to create vibrancy and intensity. The soldier's composed yet penetrating look may reflect Van Gogh's interest in the human condition and individual character.

Critical Reception and Legacy:
Van Gogh's depictions of Zouaves contributed to his posthumous fame, showcasing his skill in portraiture and color. While the critical reception during his lifetime was limited, modern viewers appreciate these works for their expressive use of color and texture.

Unique or Interesting Facts:
An interesting fact about Van Gogh's work during this period is that he was profoundly influenced by Japanese prints, which is evident in the bold use of color and outlined forms in this painting. Additionally, it's worth noting that Van Gogh's time in Arles was one of the most productive periods of his career, with the artist creating many of his most celebrated works during this time.

Orchard Bordered by Cypresses (1888)

Artwork Description:
"Orchard Bordered by Cypresses" is a painting by Vincent van Gogh featuring a lively orchard in bloom. The scene is set against a vivid blue sky with towering cypresses flanking the edges, creating a natural frame. Van Gogh's use of contrasting colors and dynamic, directional brushstrokes captures the vibrancy of spring and the lushness of the blooming trees.

Historical Context:
This work was painted in 1888 while Van Gogh was living in Arles, in the South of France. The region's intense light and color significantly influenced his work, leading to the creation of some of his most celebrated paintings. Van Gogh was particularly taken with the Provençal landscape, which he found to be an endless source of inspiration.

Symbolism and Interpretation:
The orchard in bloom can be seen as a symbol of new life and hope, themes that were personally significant to Van Gogh as he sought refuge from his mental anguish through his art. Cypresses, often associated with mourning in Western art, are presented here in a more positive light, possibly symbolizing eternal life or the constancy of nature.

Critical Reception and Legacy:
Van Gogh's work was largely unrecognized during his lifetime, but his posthumous fame grew rapidly. Today, paintings like "Orchard Bordered by Cypresses" are highly valued for their emotional depth and innovative technique. This painting, like many from his period in Arles, contributed to the foundation of modern art.

Unique or Interesting Facts:
Van Gogh created several series of orchard paintings, capturing different stages of bloom and times of day. This pursuit reflects his interest in the Japanese practice of creating variations on a single theme, a technique he adapted and made his own. Additionally, Van Gogh's use of the orchard motif was part of his larger goal to create a series of works that could form a decorative ensemble, reflecting his interest in art's ability to beautify and uplift the human spirit.

Tree Roots in a Sandy Ground (1882)

Artwork Description:
This early drawing shows Van Gogh's interest in the natural world and the details of plant life. The work is executed in ink on paper and portrays a complex tangle of tree roots exposed above the ground, with the absence of the tree's canopy suggesting a focus on the unseen aspects of nature.

Historical Context:
Created during Van Gogh's stay in The Hague, this work predates his more famous period in France. It shows his early exploration of themes and techniques that would later become central to his art, such as the expressive potential of lines and the emphasis on nature's raw elements.

Symbolism and Interpretation:
The twisting, gnarled roots might be seen as symbolic of struggle and growth, themes that Van Gogh would revisit throughout his career. This piece can also be interpreted as a study in form and texture, elements that Van Gogh believed were essential to depicting the essence of his subjects.

Critical Reception and Legacy:
Van Gogh's early drawings were overshadowed by his later paintings, but they are now appreciated for their raw beauty and the insight they provide into his developing artistic vision. His drawings are considered a significant part of his oeuvre, demonstrating his skills in observation and his unique approach to line and texture.

Unique or Interesting Facts:
Van Gogh's drawings from this period were often created as studies for paintings or as exercises in technique. This work, with its detailed rendering of the roots, shows a meticulous and patient observation that characterizes much of Van Gogh's early work. It is a testament to his lifelong fascination with nature and the resilience of life.

Flower Beds in Holland (1883)

Artwork Description:
This early work ("Flower Beds in Holland" also known as "Bulb Fields ") of Van Gogh is a depiction of the tulip fields of Holland, showcasing rows of colorful blooms against a rural backdrop. It's notable for its bright, contrasting colors and the way it captures the essence of spring.

Historical Context:
This painting was created before Van Gogh developed his signature Post-Impressionistic style. During this period, he was influenced by the Dutch tradition of landscape painting and was also inspired by the burgeoning modern agricultural industry in the Netherlands.

Symbolism and Interpretation:
The painting can be seen as a symbol of growth and renewal, common themes in Van Gogh's work. The meticulous rows of flowers could also reflect his search for order in nature, a contrast to the emotional turmoil he often experienced.

Critical Reception and Legacy:
While Van Gogh was not well-known during his lifetime, his works gained immense popularity posthumously. "Flower Beds in Holland" is an example of his early work that hints at the vibrant use of color that would become a hallmark of his later, more famous pieces.

Unique or Interesting Facts:
Van Gogh's fascination with the agricultural landscapes of his homeland persisted throughout his career. This painting stands out as one of the few works from his early period where he experimented with the vivid color contrasts that would later define his most celebrated works.

Self-Portrait Dedicated to Paul Gauguin (1888)

Artwork Description:
This painting is one of the many self-portraits by van Gogh. It features the artist with a stern expression, set against a vibrant green background. Van Gogh's intense gaze and the stark contrasts of the green against his ginger hair and blue clothes make this painting striking.

Historical Context:
Van Gogh painted this self-portrait during his time in Arles, France, a period when he was anticipating the arrival of Paul Gauguin. He intended this portrait as a gift for Gauguin as part of his efforts to establish a community of artists.

Symbolism and Interpretation:
Self-portraits were a significant part of van Gogh's work, often reflecting his psychological state. The use of contrasting colors and the confrontational gaze might symbolize the complex and tumultuous nature of van Gogh's personality and life.

Critical Reception and Legacy:
During his lifetime, van Gogh was not commercially successful. However, his self-portraits have since become iconic, recognized for their emotional depth and innovative techniques. They have contributed significantly to the image of van Gogh as a tortured artist.

Unique or Interesting Facts:
It's known that van Gogh painted this self-portrait as a part of a series of portraits exchanged with Gauguin. The intense and almost confrontational nature of the self-portrait reflects the complicated relationship between the two artists. The portrait's thick, swirling brushstrokes are characteristic of van Gogh's signature style and are believed to have been influenced by Japanese prints, which both artists admired.

Vase with Twelve Sunflowers (1889)

Artwork Description:
The painting depicts a vase containing a vibrant collection of sunflowers. With a palette of deep yellows, greens, and a contrasting blue background, van Gogh's thick and expressive brushwork gives the flowers a tactile quality. The sunflowers are at different stages of their life cycle, from full bloom to withering, adding a poignant note to the painting.

Historical Context:
Van Gogh painted a series of sunflower paintings to decorate his house in Arles, in anticipation of a visit from his friend and fellow artist, Paul Gauguin. The sunflowers had special significance for van Gogh, representing gratitude and symbolic of his search for meaning and light.

Symbolism and Interpretation:
Sunflowers were significant to van Gogh as a symbol of happiness and artistic inspiration. They are often interpreted as reflecting van Gogh's fascination with the cycles of life and nature's transience, as well as his quest for light and truth in his work.

Critical Reception and Legacy:
Van Gogh's sunflower paintings have become some of his most famous and beloved works, celebrated for their vibrant color and emotional depth. They were not widely known during his lifetime but gained immense popularity after his death, influencing generations of artists.

Unique or Interesting Facts:
Van Gogh created several sunflower paintings during his lifetime, each with a unique composition and mood. The sunflower series showcases his revolutionary use of yellow and his ability to imbue simple subjects with intense emotional resonance. These works have become synonymous with van Gogh's legacy and are considered some of the most iconic images in Western art.

Portrait of Dr. Gachet (1890)

Artwork Description:
"Portrait of Dr. Gachet" is a compelling image of Vincent van Gogh's physician, Dr. Paul Gachet, who looked after the artist in the final months of his life. The portrait is noted for its emotional intensity; Dr. Gachet's melancholic expression is rendered in somber colors with poignant touches, such as the clasped hands and the contemplative gaze. The use of swirling patterns in the background and the contrasting colors accentuate the emotional depth of the subject.

Historical Context:
Van Gogh painted this portrait shortly after his release from the Saint-Rémy asylum and only weeks before his death in July 1890. Dr. Gachet was known to be sympathetic to artists and had a personal interest in art himself. Van Gogh's time in Auvers-sur-Oise was both productive and turbulent, with the artist creating numerous paintings, including this portrait.

Symbolism and Interpretation:
The portrait is often seen as a reflection of the empathy Van Gogh felt for Dr. Gachet, who was himself struggling with melancholy. The presence of the digitalis plant, traditionally used to treat heart conditions, can be seen as a symbol of healing and care. The painting is also interpreted as a representation of the shared understanding of suffering between the artist and his doctor.

Critical Reception and Legacy:
"Portrait of Dr. Gachet" is one of Van Gogh's most revered portraits, achieving fame both for its artistic mastery and the tragic context of its creation. It has been sold for record-breaking prices at auction and remains a subject of fascination for its complex portrayal of the sitter.

Unique or Interesting Facts:
There are two known versions of this portrait, each with slight variations in color and detail. The painting became the subject of a legal controversy after Dr. Gachet's son disputed its authenticity, although it is now widely accepted as genuine. The portrait's record sale price of $82.5 million in 1990 set it apart as one of the most expensive paintings ever sold at the time.

A Walk along the Banks of the Seine near Asnières (1887)

Artwork Description:
This painting captures a serene moment along the Seine River, with figures leisurely strolling or standing under the shade of trees. The vibrant blue and yellow hues reflect Van Gogh's exploration of color during his Paris period, while the dynamic brushstrokes convey the movement of the foliage and the river's surface.

Historical Context:
During his time in Paris, Van Gogh was exposed to the works of the Impressionists and post-Impressionists, which greatly influenced his style. The light colors and the depiction of modern life in this painting reflect these influences.

Symbolism and Interpretation:
The scene is a juxtaposition of nature and the urban environment, highlighting the peaceful coexistence of the two. The trees serve as a natural canopy over the promenade, symbolizing a sheltered path or journey.

Critical Reception and Legacy:
Van Gogh's paintings from his Paris period were critical in his development as an artist. While not widely recognized during his lifetime, his works, including this one, are now praised for their innovative use of color and brushwork.

Unique or Interesting Facts:
Van Gogh often ventured into the outskirts of Paris to paint. "A Walk along the Banks of the Seine near Asnières" reflects his interest in capturing the everyday activities of people and the landscape around them. This painting is part of a series of works that Van Gogh created focusing on the Seine and the people enjoying their leisure time beside it.

Wheatfield with Poppies and Lark (1887)

Artwork Description:
This work depicts a serene landscape with a vast field of wheat, speckled with red poppies and under an expansive blue sky. A lark can be seen in the sky, adding a sense of life and movement to the scene.

Historical Context:
This painting was created during Van Gogh's time in Paris when he was heavily influenced by Impressionism and Japanese prints. It was a period of experimentation and transition, leading to the development of his unique style characterized by vibrant colors and dynamic brushstrokes.

Symbolism and Interpretation:
The poppies may symbolize sleep, peace, or death, which are recurring themes in Van Gogh's work. The lark is often seen as a symbol of hope and spiritual ascent. Together, they may represent the juxtaposition of life and death, a theme that Van Gogh often explored.

Critical Reception and Legacy:
Van Gogh's work was not widely known or celebrated during his lifetime, but his posthumous recognition grew rapidly. Today, his paintings are celebrated for their emotional depth and beauty. This particular painting shows Van Gogh's love for nature and his ability to convey emotion through landscape.

Unique or Interesting Facts:
Van Gogh often painted wheat fields, which held special significance for him as symbols of life and rebirth. The presence of the lark, a bird that sings as it soars, is significant as Van Gogh enjoyed the symbolism of birds in flight, which may represent freedom or escape.

Wheatfield with Crows (1890)

Artwork Description:
This painting is often noted for its haunting beauty, featuring a vibrant yellow wheatfield under a turbulent sky, populated by a flock of crows. It is one of Van Gogh's most famous and powerful images, and one of his last works.

Historical Context:
"Wheatfield with Crows" was painted during the artist's time in Auvers-sur-Oise, near Paris, where he moved for the fresh country air and to be under the care of Dr. Gachet after his release from the asylum in Saint-Rémy.

Symbolism and Interpretation:
There is much debate among art historians about the symbolism of this painting. Some see the crows and the dark sky as ominous signs reflecting Van Gogh's troubled state of mind. The three separate paths can be interpreted as symbolic of Van Gogh's uncertainty about the future.

Critical Reception and Legacy:
While Van Gogh was not commercially successful during his lifetime, this painting, like many of his others, grew in esteem over time. Today, it is viewed as a masterpiece and a profound expression of human emotion and the artist's psychological state.

Unique or Interesting Facts:
This work is often thought to be Van Gogh's last painting, although this is not certain. The dramatic, swirling sky and the path that seems to lead nowhere have led many to associate the painting with the artist's impending death. Some interpretations suggest that the crows represent the darkness coming over Van Gogh's life, while others see them simply as part of the landscape he was depicting.

Willows at Sunset (1888)

Artwork Description:
"Willows at Sunset" is a vibrant painting that illustrates a sunset landscape. It features the silhouette of willow trees against a strikingly luminous sky with the sun depicted as a radiant orb. The ground is rendered in vivid shades of orange and yellow, suggesting the reflection of the sunset's glow.

Historical Context:
Van Gogh painted "Willows at Sunset" during his time in Arles, France, where he was inspired by the landscape and light of the region. This period was one of the most productive and innovative in his career, as he worked towards developing his signature style.

Symbolism and Interpretation:
The willows, with their elongated forms reaching upwards, could be interpreted as symbols of aspiration or resilience. The setting sun might represent the end of a cycle or the transient nature of life, themes Van Gogh often pondered.

Critical Reception and Legacy:
While Van Gogh was not commercially successful during his lifetime, his work posthumously received widespread acclaim. Paintings like "Willows at Sunset" contribute to the appreciation of his talent in capturing the essence and emotion of a scene through color and brushwork.

Unique or Interesting Facts:
Van Gogh's use of swirling patterns in the sky and the vivid, contrasting colors are characteristic of his works from the Arles period. The technique used in this painting would later evolve into the iconic style seen in his famous "Starry Night." The use of directional brushstrokes to convey movement and emotion demonstrates Van Gogh's innovative approach to landscape painting.

Related Books include the following:

Van Gogh's Vibrance: A Picture Book for the Mind and Soul

ISBN: 9798850567040
ASIN: B0C9S7FR8B

Vincent's Visions: A Tapestry of Art and Words
Celebrating the Legacy of van Gogh through Color and Verse

ISBN: 9798857692158
ASIN: B0CFCY7HQ5

Related Books include the following:

Ruled Notebook - Irises:
Vincent van Gogh Renowned
Painting | A Gift Book for
Writing on Lined Paper
Paperback – October 11, 2021

ASIN: B09JBMR9WQ
ISBN: 979-8494210562

Ruled Notebook – Sunflowers:
Vincent van Gogh 1889
Masterpiece Painting | A Book
of Lined Pages for Taking Notes
Paperback – October 31, 2021

ASIN: B09KN65ZYD
ISBN: 979-8756703337

Printed in Great Britain
by Amazon